# Warp & Weft

# WARP & WEFT

### Kim Taplin

*Warp & Weft*
Kim Taplin

Published by Aspect Design 2021
Malvern, Worcestershire United Kingdom
Tel: 01684 572850
Email: allan@aspect-design.net
Web: www.aspect-design.net

Author's email: kimtaplin1@gmail.com

Designed, printed and bound by Aspect Design
89 Newtown Road, Malvern, Worcs. WR14 1PD
United Kingdom
Tel: 01684 561567
E-mail: allan@aspect-design.net
Website: www.aspect-design.net

ISBN 978-1-912078-07-3

*For Foni, Efi and Bella*

# Contents

# About the Poet

Kim Taplin was born in Oxford and raised on the edge of the New Forest, near Southampton. He studied theology and education at the Universities of Oxford and Cambridge. He has worked as a teacher, a supermarket assistant, a parish priest, a lavatory cleaner, a public school chaplain and a car park attendant. He is a FRSA. Kim enjoys walking in the Malvern Hills, reading modern Greek literature, supporting Southampton Football Club, sampling real ales and pottering in his garden. He and his Greek wife, Chryssa, live in Great Malvern. *Warp & Weft* is his first volume of poetry.

# Genesis Moment

In primal darkness
diffused with cosmic light,
our ancestral ocean-born creature,
bemused by current and surf,
lies out-of-depth upon the shore,
facing that momentous decision –
to sand-slide back, sea-bound,
or to gasp for air
and see what happens next.

# Dotting the I's

He assembled flat-packs
with military precision,
in close order,
dutifully obedient to detail.
Shelves never out of step,
and no treacherous nuts or bolts
absent without leave.

He followed recipes
to the letter,
with all ingredients to scale;
nothing out of balance.
No illicit herbs or spices.
Serving time – forty minutes
(180 degrees, 160 fan).

He always left home
with a GPS tracker,
a compass and a map.
Never lost,
(though often absent),
he couldn't see the hills
for the contours.

Never straying off-path,
he lived his risk-free days
with fences unhurdled and trees untopped;
games unfrolicked and riddles unsolved;
kisses unstolen and stories untold;
answers unquestioned and visions unseen.

## Ways and Means

Don't curse
but bless the path,
for turnings missed, for signs
unclear and trackings back, anxious
to find

your home.
And, safely there, you'll understand –
when setting out there are
no ends, just ways
and means.

## Three in One

The Ground of all that is; the Source of Light;
transcendent Lord of Hosts beyond compare,
yet paradox of loving grace and might.

Our god-born man who freely chose to bear
a scapegoat's yoke (though he was not to blame),
so humankind divinity could share.

Pure, gentle breath which fans a sacred flame
within my wounded soul shall it inspire
to learn, to laugh, to love and to proclaim

a Trinity of life and blood and fire.

# Africa Star

*In memoriam*
*Signalman G. T. J. Taplin, Royal Corps of Signals*
*D Troop, 1 Squadron, 10th Armoured Division Signals (Middle East Force)*

His khaki, canvas wallet
bleached by Ra in Pharaoh's Land,
opened for the very first time
in threescore years and ten.
Stuffed to the stitches with fading photos
of comrades-in-arms, Arabic stamps
and Alexandria's unused change.

And a *Kalender* (1942) in desert-yellow,
*Panzergruppe Afrika*
proudly embossed on the cover,
with swastika superimposed
on a palm of dates –
battle flotsam from an ocean of sand.
Swapped or recovered?
Too late to ask.

And in my father's pencilled hand,
a list of patriotic sing-along songs,
motorcycle maintenance tips
and unfinished poems
offering a glimpse
of the man at twenty-one.

A soldier lamenting that
'There are so many; some have seen
The war-scarred lives of Alamein.'

A son yearning for mother and home;
for it all to come to an end:
'Christmas '43 has passed,
The year is almost finished.
The year that was to be the last
Has left our hopes diminished.'

And now, this other son sits and wonders
what the next verse might have been.

# Bee's Purple

Man understands he's not so wise
When Nature takes him by surprise –
For instance, ultraviolet light
Is visible to bees in flight.

But we are blind to such array
And miss bright visions every day;
Rich colours of the deepest hue
Like reddest red and bluest blue.

Perhaps we humans need to learn,
There's much of life we can't discern,
So we should bow and bend a knee
To laud the humble bumble bee.

# A Tale of Two Civilisations

Once upon a time, Mythos roamed freely across the earth. She was welcomed wherever she wandered. Her stories were shared in caves and around campfires, they were rehearsed in hamlets and villages. Even in the town, Mythos was ever-present; she entertained in hostelries, nurtured in homes, healed in hospitals and offered hope in the hospice. Mythos was always clothed in the multi-coloured, flowing robes of Imagination, and Narrative was her mother tongue.

Then one day, Logos arrived in town. He sported a crisp, modern suit of Reason and he spoke a strange dialect called Theory. The people flocked to hear him and, before long, they too were speaking Theory. In the fullness of time, the town became the city. Its inhabitants changed their names to numbers and they occupied geometric, story-proof tower blocks. Meanwhile, Mythos became homeless.

After a time, the citizens began to miss Mythos. Logos had taught them *how* to live but he couldn't explain to them *why*. So, the citizens searched far and wide for Mythos. They eventually found her on the margins, in the hinterland, squatting in crumbling theatres and redundant places of worship. She had been befriended by children, artists, poets and those painfully addicted to meaning.

So, Mythos was led back home, where she was welcomed with open minds. When the time was ripe, love blossomed between Logos and Mythos and they were joined together forever in a ceremony called Truth.

# Invictus

Under September's milky sun
lie newborn seeds of buffed mahogany,
rent full-term
from green-spiked, warty wombs.

And taken by surprise,
I'm nine again –
this timorous schoolboy
preparing for combat;
scrabbling around for
that elusive gladiator.
The unconquerable.

# Lost Dream

She rarely remembered
her nightmares.
But that morning,
in the shower,
she was swept away
in torrents of grief
as she recalled
not the memory,
nor the meaning,
but the feeling
of the dream.

# Emmanuel

He could bear it no longer.
So, he vacated his executive seat
high up in the stand,
ran down to the touchline,
pulled on the team's shirt,
laced up his boots
and joined in the game.

## Incarnation

Infinity as Man, flesh-dressed,
almighty, nursing at the breast;
unlimited, yet crib-confined,
eternal new-born of our kind;
an exile, though of kingly state,
a scent of myrrh divines his fate;
the Prince of Sorrows unsurpassed.
His path is set. The die is cast.

# Sine Spe Recuperandi

On the motorway hard shoulder
between average speed check
and services sixteen miles,
jetsam cast adrift
lies marooned in despair of salvage –
one-use plastic bags,
an empty cola bottle,
the shredded slithers of a lorry tyre
and a solitary traffic cone,
neglected and abused,
expelled from distant serried ranks,
with no worthwhile future employment.

Between variable speed limit
and tiredness can kill take a break,
unintended flotsam
lies with no hope of recovery –
the fox and the badger who almost made it
and a single shoe pining for its twin,
as in Cinderella, but with
no happy ending.

# Seasons

[i] Summer (*Ficus carica*)

A fulsome fig tree
Fan-trained against the brickwork,
Blue-purple sweetness.

[ii] Autumn (*Aesculus hippocastanum*)

A horse chestnut sheds
Auburn seeds on the asphalt,
No hope of rooting.

[iii] Winter (*Vitis vinifera*)

An unleafed grape vine
Snow-dressed on a steel wire frame,
Fruit long forgotten.

[iv] Spring (*Helianthus annuus*)

A bright sunflower
Cracks open its concrete tomb,
Resurrection life.

# Primary

She painted by instinct.
Broad brushstrokes
oozing colour
on boundless, eager canvasses;
sublime impressions in gouache,
acrylic and oil,
her palette revelling
in viridian, yellow ochre,
burnt sienna and ultramarine.

At art college,
they taught her the correct techniques
and how to pass an exam.
So, listening and unlearning,
she became confined within her frames,
tormented by tones and tints,
tentatively applying
only primary colours.
She painted by numbers
the rest of her life.

## The King's Shilling

He'd only just arrived at the front –
one of Kitchener's boys,
in splatter-free virgin khaki
and Tommy's helmet,
uniform and undented
from no near misses.

He stood tauntingly tall
in the mud-swamped trench,
wide-eyed and petrified,
clutching his Lee-Enfield
(bayonet fixed),
waiting for the whistle. It came
in a moment.

He barely made it over the top.
No chance of an heroic death.
No chance of glory.
No chance.
His war
was
just
one
shot.

# God-in-a-Box

Mother Church laboured two millennia
in her quest to define God –
convening councils;
convoking conclaves;
concocting creeds.

But no matter how systematically
she sought to classify the divine,
she still couldn't make her doctrines
fit neatly together,
without remainder.

Like an overfull suitcase,
there is always
an inconvenient                    bit of truth
bulging untidily
out of the side.

## French Lesson

'Encore une fois!' Yet once more, from the start,
we stammer through the names of all *les mois*,
but never try to learn those months by heart.
'Encore une fois!'

Madame had not an inkling we *trente-trois*
were playing hard-to-learn, and deemed it smart
to answer in franglais and crude *patois*.

A teacher now, with knowledge to impart,
I fear my younger self was *discourtois*
and yearn to make amends, at least in part,
*encore une fois.*

# Tuning in

Hear my lyrics,
but please listen to my music too.
However, be warned –
I'm not easy-listening mood music,
nor soporific supermarket piped music,
nor even please hold the line
your call is important to us music.
Follow my melody and harmony,
if you will.
Discern the bass line,
if you can.
But only when you sense the dissonance,
will you know
you're on the right track.

## Croeso i Gymru

Westbound on the Severn Bridge,
to the fringe where Celts are bred,
homeland of the dragon's fire,
male voice choir and rugby-red.

Snowdon's peak and leek-green hills,
daffodils and Gower sand,
coastal path and steely sea –
Oh, to be in Dewi's Land!

# In Perpetuity

I've paid the mortgage off;
this house is mine.
I own its swathe of land –
six hundred metres square,
freehold (no restrictive covenants).
Nine thousand bricks and lime,
arranged in the Victorian style,
with compact, paved courtyard to rear
(only partially overlooked),
anonymous shrubs, assorted herbs
and a lonely olive in exile.

But one day I shall leave;
too old to climb the stairs,
forgetful of my name,
they'll move me to another home
(it'll be for the best, they'll say)
with thirty more who used to boast
of paltry patches of planet,
leased for a while.

And some time hence,
reluctantly,
I'll own four more cubic metres of soil,
and my other home will return to earth
with a few forgotten broken bricks
hinting at what once belonged to me,
freehold and mortgage free.

Then, that scorched, neglected ground
will barely be the pride of goats,
with so few inhabitants left
to own anything
but nostalgia
and regret
for missed opportunities.

# Across the Bar

I catch your eye and you catch mine,
we look away to sip our wine.
A further glimpse, a furtive glance –
perhaps it's time to take a chance.
Once more we peek, a hopeful plea
from me to you and you to me.
I arch my brow. You smile. No doubt.
We'll take the risk, we're both found out.

# Childhood Solutions

She worked out
that Daddy was Father Christmas
because Santa couldn't afford any presents
that year.
She realised
that Mummy was the Tooth Fairy
when she didn't have any loose change
in her purse.
She discovered
that Grandma was the Easter Bunny
as she spotted her hiding chocolate eggs
in the garden.

She's thirty-two now . . .
but she still hasn't solved the problem
of the Baby Jesus.

# On the Touchline

He was the only dad on the touchline.
In gunmetal coat and auburn shiny shoes,
through countless hours and miles,
still he was there,
the only dad on the touchline.

Why did I pretend not to see him?
Why did I hide amongst the team?
Why was the walk across adolescent
no-man's-land too shameful?

'I thought my shoes were dirty,'
he said in the kitchen,
as I eavesdropped from two rooms away.

Even now, as I write,
his disappointment still aches,
as his shoes were always polished
and all that was scuffed
was my soul.

# The Elect

*Manchester United 9 – 0 Southampton*
*(Premier League, 2nd February 2021)*

In the picking of teams,
captain cocksure
disdains alternate choice
and imposes his might to decide.
And so we, the sad unselected,
are beaten black and blue
by his squad of school colours,
with just one attainable goal
(on such lopsided turf) –
to limit the score
to single figures.

Even top flight winners
are chosen before kick off
by distant billionaires,
while Canaries, Magpies and Eagles
languish in pyrite cages
and Saintly south coast misfits
shiver on the touchline,
sullenly staring at their boots,
still hoping to keep the score down.

# Three Letter Demolition

You sense it coming
from her very first word,
with that patronising tone,
eye-free smile
and the faintest of praise.
Then, right on cue,
the dreaded
*But*
swings in like a wrecking ball,
smashing down your walls,
sending your constructions
crashing to the ground.

# School Rules

'This school has only two rules,'
announced the new headmaster,
brimming with educational innovation.
'One – Act sensibly.
Two – Keep to the left in the corridors.'

Sanctioned for anarchy,
we discovered, by break time,
that chewing gum was not acting sensibly.
Nor was dropping litter.
And by the end of the day,
it wasn't sensible to talk in lessons,
or to lose your P.E. kit,
or to fart in French,
or to pull Helen Brown's hair
(though she did say I was fat!).

By half term, the Head thought it sensible
to innovate a shiny red booklet
of sixty-three regulations
defining rule one.

Decades on,
I still keep to the left in corridors.

# On Malvern Hills

The short path leads to St Ann's Well,
across the dell;
on ancient ground,
we're Beacon bound!
Then, near the trig point, flaked with snow,
it's hard to know
which aspect's best –
east, south or west.
Reluctant to forego such views,
we gladly choose
the long path down
back into town.

# Kintsugi

*Kintsugi is the five hundred-year-old Japanese art of repairing broken pottery with lacquer dusted or mixed with powdered gold, silver or platinum. It values breakages and skilled repairs as part of a pot's history; something to be cherished rather than disguised. Philosophically, Kintsugi suggests we should embrace our human fragility and imperfections.*

This broken tea pot
Golden-dusted in repair
Joins our outpoured lives
Fractured fragmented and flawed
Yet beautiful to behold

# Tea Dance

She graciously accepts his invitation,
and between Red Cross sandwiches
and cups of insipid Ceylon tea,
they waltz, foxtrot and quickstep
until the Argentine Tango
tangles them for ever.

Far too soon, the spell is broken;
through a party wall,
the insistent assault
of drum 'n' bass
invades his ballroom.
So, he sacramentally replaces
the crimson crêpe chiffon dress
on its satin padded hanger
in her side of the wardrobe
and clicks the bedroom door
shut.

Stepping down gingerly
a stair at a time,
he sits in her kitchen
with his memories
and makes
tea for one.

# Between Fire and Light

The gift imparting vision without sight
Shall turn our faces to the sacred fire,
To raise our souls from shadow into light.

In umbral flame candescent in the night,
Within yet far, we let go to acquire
The gift imparting vision without sight.

In awe, we offer thanks as we delight
In Nature's alms – the bounty we require
To raise our souls from shadow into light.

To dare declare dire wrong from noble right,
May Lady Justice teach us to desire
The gift imparting vision without sight.

We question, 'Why the perils of our plight?'
And yet, despite despair, we still aspire
To raise our souls from shadow into light.

Great Mystery of Love, opaque yet bright,
With yearning and in wonder we admire
Your gift imparting vision without sight,
That raises souls from shadow into light.

# American Kestrel

Snubbing his handler's mousy bribe,
*Falco sparverius* veered left,
exercising a predator's
right to decide.

Alighting halfway,
on an unsuspecting human perch,
his tender yet taut talons on my thigh
half-hinted that such intimate homage
may only fleetingly be rendered
to pastel slate-blue
and rich rust-red
and black-speckled white,
dusted with cinnamon.

Was it my coat of forage-green
that held him rapt?
Or, perhaps, he simply sensed
my long-jessed soul meant well enough
to confer on me
this highest of honours.

# Words Count

When *Word* was young, she enjoyed dressing up as signs and symbols. She loved playing sentences with her friends. Then, one day, she was invited to join in storytime and she knew she had discovered her destiny. Mere messages were no longer satisfying; myths and meaning beckoned. So she studied herself in context and eventually graduated in concepts.

As the years passed, *Word* discarded her threadbare garments of hieroglyphs, cuneiform and manuscript. She abandoned her old haunts of bone, stone, clay, papyrus and vellum, resolving to make a successful career in codices, first editions and paperbacks. She was awarded numerous prizes for her achievements in philosophy and literature.

However, over time, *Word* lost definition. She became outnumbered and marginalised. There were now centillions of electronic words and few cared anymore for meaning or myth; messages (half-true and false) became all-pervasive. Ominously, on her final page, *Word* was forced to take a humble position in information, with the existential threat of a role in data.

## The Poet and the Fisherboy

Gentle Greek
fingers fumble with
reel and rod.
Hopes of paternal pride
tangled in knots of nylon,
as circling shoals
taunt and tease.

Meanwhile, the watching poet
casts for winsome words,
but catches only alliteration
with such beguiling bait
so simply stolen from the hook.

# St Dunstan-in-Olympus

*Persephone Eleanor Beattie, born 2nd September 2010*

In Church Street's terraced home, on holy ground,
We crouch, enthralled in reverential love
And as we gaze you utter not a sound,
Reposing like a goddess from above.
Few hours ago you scarcely had a name
(in dark maternal womb; your time to wait),
But now contingent light sets you aflame
With hopeful dreams and vagaries of fate.
Who are you now, and who will you become,
Our maiden-child of miracle and myth?
Spring-bearer, to the winter ne'er succumb
Despite six blood red *rodi* seeds and pith.

Fair *kore* of our hearts, our souls enmesh,
Persephone, our Queen, flesh of our flesh.

# Away with Words

I'm at a loss for them.
I can't find the right ones –
it's beyond them anyway.

You have a way with them,
but please don't offer them empty,
masquerading as magical,
or try to put them into my mouth.

You see, he had no last ones
(famous or otherwise),
and I can never again
come to terms.

# Victor Ludorum

[i]

On the final day of school,
he was inconsolable.
He already knew
that these were to become
*the best days of his life.*

[ii]

The time comes for every warrior
to remove his battle mask,
unfasten his armour
and let his wounds see the light of day.
Only then may healing begin –
though the scars will always remain.

# In Dymock Wood

We pass the leaning willow by the brook
and enter Dymock Wood beyond the gate,
then take the travelled path to steal a look
at Nature's springtime wonders ere too late.

Though frost has kissed the earth in April's chill
and milky flowers fade as snowflakes fall,
the lenten lilies stand – tall heads rise still,
their golden glory holding us in thrall.

We tread where poets trod in simpler days
and eavesdrop on their ghosts among the trees;
though war's vain madness set that world ablaze,
their timeless words still carry on the breeze.

# Palm Sunday

The crowds have dispersed; the air is still.
A trail of trodden palms and a few forgotten cloaks
lie scattered in the dust –
the debris of a party after the guests have gone.
And on a distant hillside,
lambs are led to Passover
and soldiers are working with wood.

# Canterbury Cathedral Gate

In the early minutes of Easter Day,
bank holiday revellers
pinball between pubs and clubs.

*He is Risen* and
*I have come that they may have fullness of life*
are chalked on the cobblestones
under their feet;
sacred-subversive graffiti
for those who have eyes to see.

Meanwhile, an officer arrests a man
full of a different spirit,
while a trio of toppling teenage girls
mouth a foul, lager-fuelled litany.
With tomorrow's amnesia,
what a great night it will have been.
Life in all its fullness.

# I Want to Be Assertive

I want to be assertive, to be there at the kill,
To send food back at restaurants, refuse to pay the bill.
I want to be assertive, I'd like to run the show,
To get an instant refund, negotiate my 'No!'

I'd stand my ground on principle, I'd always have my say,
I'd question all my boss's plans, I'd bargain for my pay,
I'd be on pole at traffic lights, I'd never queue for long,
I'd always make decisions and find I'm never wrong.

I'd like to be assertive, but know that in the end,
I'd rather be a doormat than live without a friend.

# Down to a T

There was a time
when choice definite articles
were honoured with
capital letters –
The Church,
The Monarchy,
The Government
(to name just three).

But today, the church has little capital left;
tea with the Queen is not what it used to be;
and the Government is outmanoeuvred
by the Media.

Now, The Science has been awarded
the noble prize of 'T'.
But, what if we discover there is
no The Science after all –
only sciences
comprised of models and metaphors
and equivocal meanings
(just like religion but with the maths)?

What if the lower case
is all there is left?

# Red Rose

Enchanting Queen of Flowers, you bewitch us –
inhaling your sweet, intoxicating breath,
your passionate spell binds us
to deeply-piercing thorns.
We'll tighten our grip
to make the
red run
crim
s
o
n
.

# First World Prayer

God knew I needed it
and he answered my prayer –
a SeaDemon Tsunami 66
with twin V8 1200 horse power engines
and three luxurious cabins.
Praise him, it touches forty knots!
The Lord even blessed us with a discount –
we got 35K off the price.
We can host Bible studies on deck
in the summer.

* * *

Mama, I'm squashed and I'm cold.
Mama, the dinghy has a hole in it.
Mama, my feet are wet.
　　　— We'll make it to the shore, *inshallah*.
Mama, look at that beautiful yacht going past.

## It Is What It Is

Is it really what it is?
Is that because what could have been wasn't
and, therefore, what might be isn't?

Perhaps *que sera, sera* –
whatever will be, will be.
But maybe . . . just maybe
whatever might be, could be.

# St Valentine's College

Meeting at the Freshers' Fair,
I shook your hand for far too long,
wrong-footed by your eyes and hair.
Then later, by the drinks machine,
you brushed my arm.
By accident? By design? Who knew?
You did. But much too shy to take a risk,
I hid behind my coffee cup
and two stale custard creams.

At last, with courage summoned up,
I asked you out to watch a film:
*The Deer Hunter*, released that week
(something akin to *Bambi*, so I thought).
Then, *sub fusc* in Formal Hall,
seated, temptingly, two gowns apart,
we talked and teased through three courses,
stroked wrists in passing the peas
and fell in love over port and cheese.

Once qualified
to join our hands for good,
we held them tight (and small ones too)
through golden years with silver hair
until that fateful day
you slipped through my fingers
for ill. And now I sit alone and wait,
counting down the chimes,
recalling that first Freshers' Fair.
Holding your rings.
Wringing my hands.

# Thoughts of Loss

I'm sorry for your loss.
It's *your* loss, not mine.
I shall hold your pain,
but at a safe distance because
I am an island entire of itself
and no bell tolls for me.

Our *thoughts* are with you.
Thoughts untethered
soar like songbirds,
newly-freed.
Not so *thinking*.
We can't be so easily uncaged
from our verbs.

# Rainbow

A deluge from gunmetal sky,
ricocheting off the windscreen,
wipers in double-quick time.
Then shifting solar searchlights
and escapes of belligerent blue
forecast the advent
of the covenant sign.

Noah's pride –
all present and correct,
in memory of Duke Richard's
vanquished white rose.

A smart photo foolishly boasts
of capturing the scene
through two screens.
So, stilling the car,
awe-drenched,
we gaze at a treasure too costly
for these earthenware vessels.
And we are blessed to have been
captured by the scene.

# In a Far Country

Swineherds trudge past his pigpen,
humbly homeward bound.

But the Prodigal remains,
mocking their father-myths,
relishing his pigswill cordon bleu
and chilled, vintage swine wine.

# Soul Trek

Walker
Fervent, focussed
Hiking, climbing, praying
Sacred musings, open blisters
Pilgrim

# Genetic Memory

Remember your homecoming
to the treacherous borderlands
in knarrer and longships.
Reminisce about your battles
for freedom (or death)
in Great Alexander's land
of olive, grape and fig.
Recollect how you hacked sten
from Cornish rock,
eked Macedonian harvests
out of blood-red soil
and hand-birthed ten thousand
of Holy Aidan's lambs.
Reflect on your chosen uniforms
of war, law and grace,
worn with fearful pride
in patriotic duty
and love for the divine.
Recall your paintings and poems,
you immortal children of history,
saga and myth.

And never forget –
you have lived so long;
loved so much;
but lost too soon.

# Versus Poseidon

A boy of tender years plays by the sea
and, wielding well his tools of pail and spade,
builds high a dyke of sand against the waves;
but soon the mocking surf reclaims its ground
and, breached, the broken bank returns to beach.
Then noon sun brings a student to the task:
with guile and purpose, plying her design,
she builds a flotsam scaffold tied by weeds,
with boulders bringing bulk to hold it fast.

Awoken by the youthful engineers,
a maid of middling age just shakes her head
and mourns the loss of unconstructed dreams,
of hopes and schemes laid waste upon the sand.
But as the shadows lengthen by the coast,
a stick-supported, ancient man draws near
and, sinking to his knees, he takes his place
beside the wall and works with trembling hands.
He knows Poseidon cannot be denied,
but on that shore he's building something else.

## Human Resources

I'm happy to be a hominid –
a bipedal primate
of the mammalian species
*Homo sapiens.*

I might even have been
moulded from clay
in likeness of the divine
(if the priests are to be believed).

But please, don't let me become
a human resource;
an uncountable number;
a cog in your machine.

# Pandemic Briefing

'We're all in the same boat,'
announced the minister,
white knuckles clamped
to the maple lectern.

But my mind's eye spies us
all at sea in different boats;
a flotilla of yachts and dinghies,
cruisers and kayaks,
adrift in uncharted waters,
unbuoyed up and battened down
against the encircling storm.
And as the seasick scan the horizon,
praying for that critical lifeboat,
the capsized are lost or left behind,
clinging to their wreckage.

# Parish Matters

Our vicar, Len, was loved in Larkdale Fell –
his service times would always be the same
and though he held the keys to heaven and hell,
he'd always smile and call you by your name.

He'd wet the baby's head in church and pub,
and married Wendy's niece (at eight months gone).
He'd turn out weekly for the cricket club,
though often he was caught or bowled for none.

He patched Ted's roof and painted All Saints clock,
he paid our parish quota to the pound,
he stood by Tracey, guilty in the dock
and buried pagan Pete in holy ground.

But then the bishop wanted something new
to make All Saints *a tad more up-to-date;*
he moved Len on, he ripped out every pew
and licensed young recruits called Josh and Kate.

They hung a screen to cover up the Rood,
put comfy chairs and TVs down the aisle;
drums, keyboard and guitars to stoke the mood –
a coffee lounge, to praise West London-style.

New people came to All Saints at the start,
declaring their response to God's clear call.
They ferried people in, but kept apart
and never drank a pint or bowled a ball.

Today our church is closed; beyond repair –
a place to visit when the ramblers roam.
Old Len is now retired and lives in care,
while Josh and Kate have pews inside their home.

# Warp and Weft

Colours fade with sun and age,
threadbare,
unravelling,
so many loose ends;
till all that's left is warp and weft
and the will to weave again.

# Acknowledgements

I am very grateful to many people for their support and encouragement in producing this first volume of my poetry. I am especially indebted to my friend, the poet Derek Healy, who has been a warm, wise and constructive critic, introducing me to many poetic forms and techniques. My children, Rebekah and Christopher, have offered intelligent and incisive insights from their rich artistic, dramatic and literary experience. (As a father you can only hope that your children become more accomplished than you – I rest content in that regard.) My mother loved the sounds of words and my father wrote poetry in the North African desert during the Second World War. I thank them for their genes and for so much more. I also want to acknowledge those who have been my Teachers and Mentors: Bert Taplin, Brother Melody, Apostolos Bliates, Jean Holm, Richard Hall, Bruce Hartnell and Bob Acheson. Any successes I may have achieved in my life have, in part, been due to their wisdom, guidance and love; my follies and failings I jealously guard as my own! I would also like to thank Daniel Smith and the team at Aspect Design who have led me through the process of the publication and printing of this volume. Finally, and most importantly, I would like to pay tribute to my wife, Chryssa. She has been my soul mate, best friend, muse, encourager-in-chief, guide, defender and companion throughout life. I publish this book because of her.

Two of the poems in this volume have been previously published elsewhere: 'Tea Dance' (commended) and 'Dotting the I's' have appeared in *Graffiti*.

# Index of First Lines